MISSOURI BOTANICAL GARDEN

CLIMATRON 50

MISSOURI BOTANICAL GARDEN

CLIMATRON 50

A CELEBRATION OF 50 YEARS

ESSAY BY ERIC MUMFORD

FOREWORD BY DR. PETER H. RAVEN

3-D PHOTOGRAPHY BY DAVID E. KLUTHO

MISSOURI BOTANICAL GARDEN

ST. LOUIS, MO

Funding: Publication of *Climatron: A Celebration of 50 Years* was made possible in part by a grant from the Gertrude and William A. Bernoudy Foundation.

Editor/contributing writer: Elizabeth McNulty

Designer: Jamie Cendroski Vishwanat

Additional research by: Mary Reid Brunstrom, Andrew Colligan

Printed and bound in the United States
ISBN: 978-0-615-32591-0
Library of Congress Cataloging-in-Publication Data available upon request.
1 2 3 4 5 09 10 11 12 13

Published by: Missouri Botanical Garden
PO Box 299, St. Louis, Missouri 63166-0299
(314) 577-5100 / www.mobot.org

Distributed by: Missouri Botanical Garden Press (314) 577-9534
Big River Distribution (314) 918-9800
Purchase individual copies at the Garden Gate Shop or order online at GardenGateShop.org

PHOTO CREDITS:

Cover: *Climatron construction, November 29, 1959.* Missouri Botanical Garden Archives.

Back cover: *Climatron construction, 1960.* Missouri Botanical Garden Archives

Missouri Botanical Garden Archives: *cover, back cover,* **2** *(Rohm & Hass Reporter, vol. 30, no. 3, May/June 1961),* **5** *(assorted Climatron-related ads, articles, and ephemera),* **11**, **12**, **13**, **15**, **18**, **20**, **24**, **29**, **30**, **31**, **34**, **35**, **37**, **39**, **41**, **38**, **44** *both,* **45**, **47** *top,* **51**, **52**, **53**, **54**, **55**, **91**, **107** *top,* **108**

Lee Shannon Rhoades: **4**

Mary Lou Olson: **6**

Ian Adams: **8**, **75**

WU Photographic Services Collection, University Archives, Washington University Libraries: **14**

Joseph D. Murphy papers, St. Louis, courtesy of Caroline De Forest: **10**, **16**, **46**

Mercantile Library Collection, University of Missouri–St. Louis: **19**, **36**, **37**

Burton Historical Collection, Detroit Public Library: **21** *both*

Courtesy, the estate of R. Buckminster Fuller: **22**, **47** *bottom*

Courtesy of the Archives, California Institute of Technology: **23**

Missouri History Museum, St. Louis: **27**, **32**, **38** *top* (Ted McCrea), **38** *bottom* (Ralph D'Oench), **40** (Ted McCrea)

Courtesy of ASM International: **28**

Harris Armstrong Collection, University Archives, Washington University Libraries: **42**

Courtesy, St. Louis Abbey and Priory School: **43**

Eric Mumford: **48**

Courtesy, the Eden Project, Cornwall: **49** *top*

Flickr.com "bunnicula": **49** *bottom*

Courtesy, Mitchell Park Conservatory, Milwaukee: **50**

James P. Blair/National Geographic Image Collection **56**

Brian Mueller: **58** (*row 1: photos 1, 3*), **59** (*row 1: photo 1; row 2: photo 1; row 3: photo 4*), **69**, **81** *bottom right*

Erin Whitson: **58** (*row 1: photo 2*), **59** (*row 2: photo 2*), **63**, **66** *center,* **65** *right,* **68** *all,* **71**

Jack Jennings: **58** (*row 1: photo 4; row 2: photo 2; row 3: photos 2, 3*), **59** (*row 1: photo 4*), **76** *left*

Charles Schmidt: **58** (*row 2: photo 3*)

Matt Bender: **58** (*row 2: photo 3*), **62** *right*

Christine Seibert: **58** (*row 2: photo 4*), *back flap*

Leslie Wallace: **58** (*row 3: photo 1*), **59** (*row 3: photos 1, 2, 3*), **74** *bottom,* **79** *left,* **80** *top right*

Heather Marie Osborn: **58** (*row 3: photo 4*), **62** *left,* **65** *left,* **73**, **81** *bottom left*

Ryan Rumberger: **59** (*row 1: photo 2*), **70** *left*

Terry Rishel: **59** (*row 1: photo 3*)

Paul Straatmann: **60**, **61**, **67**, **82**, **86**, **87**, **89** *bottom*

Kevin Wolf: **64** *left,* **72** *bottom left,* **74** *top left, and right,* **81** *top right*

Jennifer Meinhardt: **64** *right,* **72** *top right,* **78**, **80** *bottom right*

Todd Gilbert: **66** *left,* **79** *bottom right,* **80** *left*

Heather Arora: **70** *top right*

Josh Monken: **72** *top left,* **90** *center circle*

Emily Snider: **72** *bottom right*

Jean McCormack: **76** *center*

JJ Lane: **77** *right*

Jami Ford: **79** *top right*

Flickr.com "Seanosh": **84** *right*

Robert LaRouche, 1990 *St. Louis Post-Dispatch:* **83**

Robert Srenco © 2009 Srenco photography: **85** *top*

Kathryn Lebbon: **85** *bottom,* **90** *tokens*

Dan Levin: **88** *left*

Rodolfo Vásquez: **88** *right*

Jack Regalado: **89** *top*

Cindy Lancaster: **90** *flower*

Flickr.com: **90** (montage, *clockwise from top:* "Bill Ward's Brickpile," "Smart Destinations," "Paul Mannix,"), "dungodung" *Statue of Liberty*

ron labbe/studio 3D: **93** *graphics,* **107**

David E. Klutho © 2010: **93–105**, **107** *bottom*

Jamie Cendroski Vishwanat: **107** *right*

To view outtakes of the Climatron 3-D photography, visit **www.climatron.org**.

To view more archival photos of the Missouri Botanical Garden, visit the Illustrated History section of the Garden's website, **www.mobot.org**.

TABLE OF CONTENTS

Foreword............6

"A rare mid-century modernist architectural gem" (A history of the Climatron)............10

    A Visionary Plantsman: Frits Went............13

    Formally and Structurally Innovative Architects: Murphy & Mackey............16

    The Original Sustainable Design Guru: Buckminster Fuller............24

    Engineering for the Future: Synergetics............32

Climatron: A Portrait............58

    Mathematics: The Numbers behind the Shapes............84

    Horticulture: A Lowland Rain Forest under Glass............86

    Science and Conservation: The Unseen Garden............88

    Climatron Trivia............90

Climatron in 3-D............92

    3-D Effects............106

Acknowledgments, Index............108

FOREWORD

The Missouri Botanical Garden, which presents a glorious display of plants for the enjoyment of the public, was built on the dreams of an extraordinary individual—Henry Shaw. An English immigrant who came to St. Louis in 1819, Shaw made his fortune selling iron objects that he imported from his uncle's factory in Sheffield and eventually other related merchandise. As he prospered, he came to dream of creating a beautiful garden for the public. Shaw ultimately made that dream his life's principal objective, adding research and education to the Garden's beauty over the 30 years he ran the institution before his death in 1889.

A century later, in the mid-twentieth century, Shaw's dream had flourished and faded. And so another dream—a dream of revitalization—was born. Director Frits Went, seeking to build a greenhouse without internal subdivisions, achieved his aim by adopting Buckminster Fuller's futuristic design of a geodesic dome. Because of the range of climates achieved within, Went called this greenhouse the "Climatron" from "climate" and *tron*, Greek for "machine." A national success when it opened in 1960, the Climatron attracted crowds back to Shaw's Garden, as the institution is affectionately called. Eventually, the Climatron's displays came to symbolize the Garden's research work in the tropics and subtropics, regions rich in plant life that are gravely threatened today.

ABOVE The Climatron holds 2,233 plants, including many rarities, but this represents less than one percent of all tropical plants. While we may preserve a few plants *ex situ* (away from their original location), we must strive to preserve biodiversity in the tropics, i.e., *in situ*, in order to protect greater numbers.

Although we depend on plants for every aspect of our lives, we are causing a large proportion of them to vanish before our very eyes. Human numbers have tripled since my own birth in the mid-1930s, and now amount to some 6.9 billion people, with another 2.5 billion projected to be added over the next few decades. This growth, combined with our rising levels of consumption, our technologies, and the associated global climate change, is causing the extinction to which we are witnesses.

Plants form the basis of human life. Through the extraordinary process of photosynthesis, a small portion of the abundant flow of energy from the sun is converted into the foundational requirements for human existence—food, clothing, shelter, fuel, beauty, medicine, and, over the course of billions of years, oxygen. Thus all life on Earth depends on plants, and we must protect them to save ourselves.

As we celebrate the 50th anniversary of the Climatron in 2010, we present its displays as a continuing manifestation of this dependency. The efforts of Missouri Botanical Garden botanists and their colleagues throughout the world provide part of the basis for the effective conservation and sustainable use of plants, and of Earth itself. Our scientists are working actively with the people of 38 nations, mostly tropical, to explore and document their plants, the uses to which they are put, and the communities in which they occur—while there is still time to do so. Please support us in this great effort!

Peter H. Raven

Dr. Peter H. Raven
President of the Missouri Botanical Garden

IN THE ECOLOGICALLY DIVERSE GROUNDS OF THE

MISSOURI BOTANICAL GARDEN IN ST. LOUIS STANDS A

RARE MID-CENTURY MODERNIST ARCHITECTURAL

GEM KNOWN AS THE CLIMATRON.

LEFT A recent view of the Climatron, designed in 1959 by St. Louis architects
Murphy & Mackey, using the geodesic dome concept of R. Buckminster
Fuller, along with the Fuller-founded engineering firm of Synergetics, Inc.

I N THE ECOLOGICALLY DIVERSE GROUNDS OF THE MISSOURI BOTANICAL GARDEN IN ST. LOUIS STANDS A RARE MID-CENTURY MODERNIST ARCHITECTURAL GEM KNOWN AS THE CLIMATRON. Based on Buckminster Fuller's geodesic dome concept, the Climatron was designed in 1959 by the local architectural firm of Murphy and Mackey, with engineers from the Fuller-founded firm of Synergetics. Its construction was part of the successful effort at the time to revitalize the Garden by its dynamic director, Frits Went, then one of the world's most influential plant scientists.

In 1976 the national American Institute of Architects named the Climatron one of the most important buildings in American architectural history, as it was the first

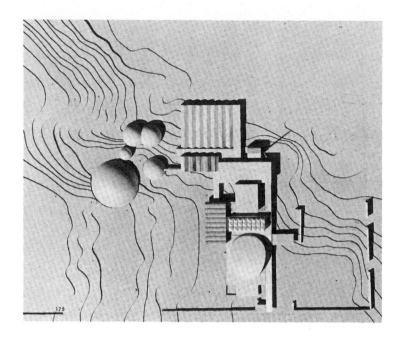

The Climatron, Missouri Botanical Garden, St. Louis, Missouri 1961

MASTER PLAN: This plan of a large portion of Shaw's Garden anticipates, in addition to the Climatron, the development of buildings for the cultivation of plant materials from the most varied and extreme climates, and for the expansion of the garden facilities into a cultural center including administrative and educational facilities, and a display pavilion foyer connecting a theater and symphony hall.
CLIENT'S NEEDS: In Phase I, a building for the cultivation and exhibition of tropical plant materials requiring a maximum of sunlight and a controlled temperature and humidity.
DESIGN SOLUTION: A large aluminum geodesic dome with a plastic skin suspended from it, providing the minimum of obstruction to sunlight, and a mechanical system designed to provide zones of differing temperature and humidity within a single enclosure. AIA- Reynolds International Competition—First Place.

RIGHT Murphy & Mackey, Missouri Botanical Garden master plan, 1961. See page 37 for more details.

geodesic dome greenhouse. It represents an unusual convergence of the ideas of two mid-twentieth century American visionaries, Fuller and Went. Although it is now mainly known as a popular place to view rare tropical plants, Went's original vision was that the new structure would be a center of scientific research on plant growth under controlled climatic conditions. Within a single column-free structure, Went planned to replicate at least four different climates, a further extension of the "phytotron" concept he had introduced as professor of botany at Caltech in Pasadena in 1949. After being recruited to lead the Garden in 1958, Went decided that building the Climatron—a term he invented—would

LEFT Missouri Botanical Garden Director Frits Went in the completed Climatron.

be a way to further extend these ideas and at the same time create a memorable public icon for the renewed Garden.

Although the Missouri Botanical Garden had been one of the leading centers for botanical research in the nineteenth century, it had fallen on hard times by the 1950s. The severe coal smoke problem in St. Louis in the 1920s had led the Garden to open another site in 1925, now called the Shaw Nature Reserve, some 35 miles farther west. Attendance at the original site had declined rapidly during the Great Depression, paralleling the decline of the city itself. When Went was given an inaugural tour of the Garden during his 1958 job interview, he found it to be a "rather depressing experience," and he noted in his diary that the aging greenhouses were in bad repair and that smog had killed off almost all the conifers. Went told Robert Brookings Smith, the chairman of the Garden Board of Trustees, that he could accept the position of Director for a "limited time only," just long enough to put the Garden back into a position of international leadership in plant research.

Went and his wife and two children drove to St. Louis from Pasadena in August 1958, moving temporarily into a house on Coffey Court in Webster Groves. Supported by the

Continued on page 14.

ABOVE Palm House, 1913. Planting palms from the D. S. Brown collection in the newly built greenhouse.

A VISIONARY PLANTSMAN

Frits Went

FRITS WARMOLT WENT (1904–1990) was the director of the Missouri Botanical Garden who commissioned the Climatron in 1959 and coined the term itself. Born in Utrecht, Holland, Went received his Ph.D. from the University of Utrecht in 1927 with a dissertation on the effects of the plant hormone auxin. He worked for a time as a plant pathologist in the research labs of the Royal Botanical Garden in Buitenzorg, Dutch East Indies (now Bogor, Indonesia) before entering academe in 1933.

He began teaching and research in the Division of Biology at California Institute of Technology, where he was among the first to demonstrate the importance of hormones in plant growth and development. He played an important role in the development of synthetic plant hormones, which then became the basis of much of the agricultural chemical industry. As part of his work at Caltech he introduced the idea of controlled climate greenhouses, which were given the name "phytotrons." His Earhart Plant Research Lab (pictured on page 23) was the first, and many others were then constructed around the world.

Went had become a world-recognized authority on plant growth when he was appointed director of the Missouri Botanical Garden in May 1958. After the opening of the Climatron, Went's vision of the Garden eventually came into conflict with that of its Board of Trustees, and he resigned in 1963. After two years as professor of botany at Washington University in St. Louis, he became director of the Desert Research Institute at the University of Nevada—Reno, where he continued his research on desert plants for the remainder of his career.

Continued from page 12.

Garden Trustees, Went soon embarked on plans to rebuild part of the Garden in time for the centennial year celebration planned for 1959. He consulted with local landscape architect Emmett Layton, and in October 1958 the Trustees commissioned two firms, Layton, Layton and Rohrbach, and architects Murphy and Mackey to develop an overall master plan for the Garden. This latter firm, founded in the early 1950s, and by this time already well established in St. Louis, had designed a series of structurally dramatic Catholic churches in the area, and in 1956 had won a limited competition to design Olin Library on the Washington University campus. (See sidebar, page 16.)

Went and Eugene Mackey got along well, and the Climatron soon became the centerpiece of the new master plan. In it, the new building would replace the 1912 Palm House and adjacent greenhouse structures, and would become the main attraction of a renewed Garden. Until that time, most of the Garden's extensive grounds were not open to visitors, and there was no guest parking. Visitors could only arrive through the pedestrian entrance along Tower Grove Avenue and visit the small number of botanical display buildings centered on the deteriorating Palm House, which opened onto a formal, Renaissance-type garden on its west side. Although both partners of Murphy and Mackey were designers and

Continued on page 19.

ABOVE Murphy & Mackey, Olin Library, Washington University, 1962. The winner of a 1956 limited competition, this building was strongly influenced by the design concepts of Le Corbusier. **RIGHT** The 1912 Palm House and the adjacent Italian Garden to the west, located on the site of the Climatron until 1958. The Doric columns from this building were retained in the Climatron until its renovation in 1990.

FORMALLY AND STRUCTURALLY INNOVATIVE ARCHITECTS

Eugene J. Mackey, Jr. (left) and Joseph D. Murphy (right)

MURPHY & MACKEY, ARCHITECTS, WAS THE ARCHITECTURAL FIRM OF RECORD IN THE CONSTRUCTION OF THE CLIMATRON.

JOSEPH DENIS MURPHY, FAIA (1907–1995) was born in Kansas City, Missouri, and educated in architecture at MIT, where he studied from 1927 to 1929. While there, he won the prestigious MIT Lloyd Warren Prize enabling him to study architecture at the École des Beaux-Arts in Paris from 1930 to 1932. Murphy launched his St. Louis career in 1938 when he and Kenneth Wischmeyer won the competition for the outdoor Municipal Opera in Forest Park. A year later he designed his family's house at 7901 Stanford in University City, which shows the influence of Finnish architect Eliel Saarinen, whose son Eero would later design the Arch. Like many of his generation, Murphy was also influenced by the work of modern architects like Le Corbusier, Oscar Niemeyer, and the German-Jewish émigré architect Eric Mendelsohn. Ultimately, Murphy was hired as the first dean of the Washington University School of Architecture in 1948, a position he held until 1952 when the demands of his growing practice required that he limit his time there.

EUGENE JOSEPH MACKEY, JR., FAIA (1911–1968) was born in Lenox, Massachusetts, and studied architecture at the Carnegie Institute of Technology (now Carnegie-Mellon University) and MIT. On the advice of Dean William Emerson of MIT, Mackey took a teaching position at Kansas State University after graduation in 1937, and from there went to teach at Washington University in St. Louis in 1941. In 1945 he won the competition to design the Court of Honor at Market and 14th Street, commemorating soldiers from St. Louis who died in World War II.

> "MACKEY DETERMINED THAT THE GEODESIC DOME WAS THE BEST WAY TO ENCLOSE THE INNOVATIVE NEW GREENHOUSE."

MACKEY AND MURPHY entered the 1947 Jefferson National Expansion Memorial competition with a scheme that called for a dramatic Mississippi River bridge. Of the 172 entries, the jury chose Eero Saarinen's Gateway Arch design.

Murphy and Mackey began practicing architecture together informally at this time, but the firm was officially founded in 1953. Their major works of the 1950s include formally and structurally innovative Catholic churches like the Resurrection Church in south St. Louis (1954) and St. Peter's, Kirkwood (1954), Bishop Du Bourg High School (1953), and many other residential, commercial, and institutional works in the area and nationally. In 1956 they won a limited competition for the new John M. Olin Library on the Washington University campus (see page 14),

North American Aviation supervisor of construction for the Climatron Albert Daufenback (left) and architect Mackey (right), 1959.

and they then designed several buildings for the Washington University Medical Center, while continuing to teach at the university.

The growing firm moved to 6124 Enright near Delmar around 1958 into a building of their own design, now demolished. It soon included firm associates Ted Wofford, who worked as a project designer with Murphy, and Harry Richman, who typically worked in a similar role with Mackey, as well as other junior architects including Eugene Mackey III and Paul Mutrux. The Climatron is the only use of a geodesic dome in their work. After Eugene J. Mackey died suddenly in 1968, the firm continued under Murphy's leadership as Murphy Downey Wofford and Richman until Murphy's death in 1995.

Continued from page 14.

sometimes worked together, for the Climatron, Mackey was the design partner who developed the concept, the result of his familiarity with Fuller's work from the latter's teaching at Washington University in 1954–55.

Went's basic idea was that the Climatron would be an experimental place for the "precise scientific study of the plant environment," allowing different species to be studied under controlled conditions. By making visible the Garden's scientific mission, it would also serve as a symbol of its new direction. Went insisted that it be a large open structure admitting as much daylight as possible, described by Mackey as a "column-free space on the side of a hill." An elaborate computer-controlled air-conditioning system, designed by St. Louis mechanical engineer Paul Londe, was planned to allow different parts of the open structure to

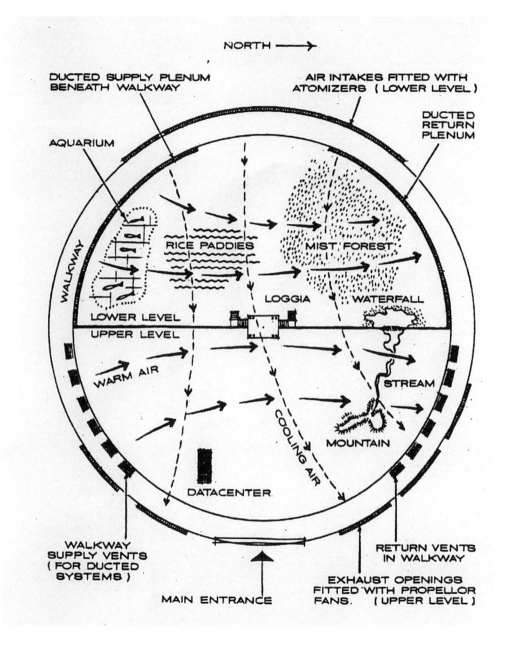

ABOVE Murphy & Mackey plan of the Climatron climate zones that were originally proposed by Frits Went (*Progressive Architecture*, April 1961).

have different climates by using large exhaust fans and water sprays. At the same time, many of the Palm House plantings and its existing split-level plan, with the western section eleven feet below the eastern half, were to be retained in the new building.

Mackey determined that Fuller's concept of the geodesic dome was the best way to cost-effectively enclose the innovative new greenhouse space. Although Went's Caltech phytotron had not been notable for its architecture, for this project Went was convinced that a transparent geodesic dome well-served what he saw as the project's most important aspect: that it provide maximum natural daylight essential to plant growth with as few columns as possible. The geodesic domes of R. Buckminster Fuller were an outgrowth of his longstanding interest in what he called the "coordinate system of nature" that organized energy patterns into logical structural systems. Fuller thought that the essence of such structures, whether natural or man-made, were triangular and tetrahedral figures (what Fuller called a "60° coordinate system") because they were the most efficient in the amount of structural material that they used.

ABOVE Climatron construction, 1959. R. Buckminster Fuller (left) tours the construction site with the Garden's executive director Dr. Hugh Cutler (center) and architect Eugene Mackey.

The term "geodesic" itself refers to a straight line on a curved surface, and is the shortest route between two points of the surface of a sphere, like the earth itself. Fuller noted that several such geodesics traced on a spherical surface intersect

to form triangular elements. (See "Mathematics," page 84.) He then experimented with variations of this idea to create structural systems that could be used in building. In 1947, he had Black Mountain College students in North Carolina make the first versions of them, and in 1951 filed for a U.S. patent on the concept. His original idea was to provide low-cost shelter, and in 1952, a model of Fuller's "geodesic house" was exhibited at the Museum of Modern Art in New York along with Frederick Kiesler's "Endless House" project. That same year Fuller was commissioned by the Ford Motor Company to build a version of such a dome over the interior of the Ford Rotunda, an exhibition and event space at Ford's corporate headquarters in Dearborn, Michigan, just outside Detroit. This pioneering translucent geodesic dome was 93 feet in diameter and constructed from an aluminum frame supporting triangular panels of polyester

ABOVE Buckminster Fuller geodesic dome at the Ford Rotunda, Dearborn, Michigan, 1953. Because the Rotunda was not able to carry a conventionally built dome, the Ford Motor Company commissioned Fuller to design a light geodesic structure of aluminum and plastic. It was destroyed by a fire that started during repairs to the plastic panels in 1962.

fiberglass over an inner tent of Orlon fabric. Ford's annual Christmas pageant, auto shows, and other spectacles made Fuller's dome the centerpiece of this popular tourist attraction, the remainder of which had been originally designed by Albert Kahn for the 1933 Century of Progress exhibition in Chicago. The Ford Rotunda unfortunately burned down completely during repairs to the dome in 1962, destroying a major example of Fuller's built work.

By using a grid of structural triangles on a spherical shape, Fuller argued that geodesic domes were the most efficient way to enclose space with a minimal amount of material. This related to Fuller's fascination with designing world systems of flows, wherein consumption of world resources would be carefully controlled, an idea he first presented with his Dymaxion World Map of 1942. He once defined "geodesic" as the "most economical relationship between any two events," and predicted in 1955 that St. Louis would become the North American center of global air travel because of the new routes over the Arctic Circle, suggesting that these would allow for a continuation of its earlier importance at the confluence of major continental river systems. These ideas

ABOVE Buckminster Fuller, Dymaxion House, Wichita, Kansas, 1945. Conceived and designed in the late 1920s, but not actually built until 1945, the Dymaxion House was one Fuller solution to the need for a mass-produced, affordable, easily transportable, and environmentally efficient house. The word "Dymaxion" was coined by combining parts of three of Fuller's favorite words: DY (dynamic), MAX (maximum), and ION (tension).

related well to Went's efforts, both at Caltech and at the Garden, to study plant growth around the world under various conditions. Both were part of mid-twentieth century efforts to organize the world with dramatic displays of new technologies and to introduce American mass audiences to the importance of the resources and geography of the rest of the world to their future.

The Climatron was not the only geodesic dome being built by the late 1950s, and many others for various purposes were also underway or completed by 1959. After receiving two large orders for experimental solid geodesic domes from the U.S. military in the early 1950s, Fuller then founded two companies to design and build them, Geodesics, Inc. and Synergetics, Inc. (See sidebar, page 32.) The latter company, based in Raleigh, North Carolina, was led by James Fitzgibbon, a North Carolina architect-engineer who also taught at Washington University as a regular visitor beginning in 1954. Fuller himself taught in a dizzying number of other design schools in the 1950s, beginning with MIT, and he constructed temporary experimental domes with students on many campuses, including several at Washington University. In addition to the

Continued on page 28.

ABOVE Caltech Earhart Plant Research Laboratories, Pasadena, California, 1961. Built in 1949, this "phytotron" was Frits Went's first effort to create a climate-controlled environment to study plant growth. It was widely imitated around the world. The buildings were razed in 1972.

THE ORIGINAL SUSTAINABLE DESIGN GURU

R. Buckminster Fuller in the Climatron

Born near Boston in Milton, Massachusetts, RICHARD BUCKMINSTER "BUCKY" FULLER (1895–1983) was an idiosyncratic self-taught engineer and designer. After dropping out of Harvard, he trained in the Navy in World War I and worked as a machinist. By the 1920s he had begun to propose radically new designs for dwellings, workplaces, and vehicles based on his investigations into the structural properties of materials. Most of these remained demonstration projects, but they acquired avant-garde cachet through his friendships with sculptor Isamu Noguchi and other modernist figures. His first book, *Nine Chains to the Moon* (1938) established Fuller as an important (if not always fully comprehensible) design theorist. Fascinated with the properties of energy flows, which he saw as the ultimate source of real wealth, he developed theories about how the structures of the physical world were patterned. His "energetic-synergetic" geometry was an effort to find what he called the "coordinate system of nature" which organized energy patterns into logical structural systems. He believed that the essence of these were triangular and tetrahedral figures, because they were the most efficient in the amount of material that they used.

During World War II, Fuller worked in industrial espionage for the U.S. government Board of Economic Warfare against the Axis. Following this experience, he began teaching at Black Mountain College in North Carolina and at the Chicago Institute of Design in 1948. These were experimental modernist schools that were receptive to his efforts to link science with design. In 1949 he became a regular visitor at MIT and then at many other university architecture schools, including Washington University in St. Louis

beginning in 1954—the same year he was awarded the U.S. patent for the geodesic dome. His initial investigations of the geodesic dome concept were inspired by efforts to find inexpensive mass housing forms, but the first built domes actually constructed were for demonstration purposes. There was a precedent for the form in the Carl Zeiss optical company's planetarium in Jena, Germany (1923), designed by an engineer, Walter Bauersfeld. This dome was photographed at the time by Laszlo Moholy-Nagy, the influential Bauhaus teacher and later founder of the Chicago Institute of Design, and Fuller was probably aware of these photos.

One of the first built Fuller domes was the Cornell University "geoscope" of 1952, where the geodesic dome became a large globe with a map of the world constructed in wire mesh on its surface. In the 1950s, Fuller's version of the dome concept became massively popular after he was commissioned to design one by the Ford Motor Company for the Ford Rotunda near Detroit in

1953 (no longer extant). This was followed by commissions for transportable domes from the U.S. Department of Defense for use by the Marine Corps and for experimental early warning radar stations ("radomes") along the Arctic Circle. Fuller then founded the firm Synergetics with James Fitzgibbon, a North Carolina State University engineer, to produce more domes. Their first commissions were for pavilions of the U.S. government abroad. These domes, commissioned by the U.S. Information Service and the U.S. Trade Agency, had a dual purpose, both to house trade shows and for use as Cold War propaganda devices to showcase American technical advances in Soviet bloc countries and around the world. The famous "kitchen debate" between Vice-President Richard Nixon and Soviet Premier Nikita Khrushchev about the relative advantages of the American capitalist versus Soviet Communist systems took place in one such dome at the American National Exhibition in Moscow in July 1959.

Fuller was appointed a research professor at Southern Illinois University in Carbondale in 1958, and in 1960 the Museum of Modern Art opened the exhibit "Three Structures by Buckminster Fuller," which featured his projects for geodesic radomes and other innovative structures. His ideas were influential for many avant-garde movements of the 1960s, including the British architect group Archigram and the

"FULLER DEFINED WEALTH AS THE TECHNOLOGICAL ABILITY TO PROTECT, NURTURE, SUPPORT, AND ACCOMMODATE ALL GROWTH NEEDS OF LIFE ON SPACESHIP EARTH."

Japanese Metabolist movement. Fuller's interest in the rational management of the world's finite resources was an inspiration to the editors of the *Whole Earth Catalog*, and in 1970 he was awarded the Nobel Peace Prize. He made many proposals for various projects in these years, though only a few of them were actually constructed. Most were better known as bold utopian visions and can be studied in his archives at Stanford University and at SIU–Carbondale. These included his and Shoji Sadao's 1960 proposal to put a giant dome over Manhattan and their 1970 "Old Man River" project, which called for a giant dome over complexes of honeycomb-like multifamily housing and commercial space in East St. Louis.

After a period of eclipse, Fuller's work has recently been rediscovered as in important progenitor of sustainable design. A major exhibition of his work was held in 2008 at the Whitney Museum in New York and traveled in 2009 to the Museum of Contemporary Art in Chicago.

Old Man River Project, 1960. Photo of a model by Buckminster Fuller for a proposed dome over East St. Louis.

Continued from page 23.

Climatron, Synergetics designed two solid all-steel domes around the same time for railway car storage, one in Baton Rouge, Louisiana (demolished) and one in Wood River, Illinois, near St. Louis. (See page 48.) Geodesic domes overseen and detailed by various other architects and engineers were also used for performing arts auditoria in Hawaii, Texas, and elsewhere. A decorative open aluminum framework dome was designed and built by Synergetics in 1960 outside the American Society of Metals headquarters near Cleveland, in Russell Center, Ohio.

The geodesic concept could be constructed out of various materials, including aluminum, wood, steel, and even cardboard, but only a few transparent domes had been built after the Ford Rotunda dome before the Climatron. Fuller himself was not directly involved in its design, however, and in early 1959, Murphy and Mackey commissioned Synergetics as the engineers for the project after Fuller had recommended them to Mackey. Fitzgibbon and Synergetics's technical representative, Pete Barnwell, who was also in charge of the solid Union Tank Car Company domes, were the main designers of the

ABOVE Synergetics, Inc., with John Kelley, architect, ASM (American Society for Metals) headquarters, Russell Center, Ohio, 2005. The open geodesic dome here was designed by the same Synergetics engineers, James Fitzgibbon and Pete Barnwell, at about the same time as the Climatron in 1959.

Climatron's actual structure, developed in close collaboration with Mackey and his firm associate Harry Richman.

Originally this design team—Mackey and Richman as the architects, and Fitzgibbon and Barnwell as the engineers—had planned to enclose the 175-foot diameter, 70-foot tall aluminum frame with a tent-like skin of clear Mylar, a new plastic fabric, but this was judged not to be durable enough. Glass panels had already been rejected as too vulnerable to breakage in hail storms, and so instead, Mackey proposed the use of clear Plexiglas. Only one-third as heavy as glass, Plexiglas was a

thermoplastic material that had been invented in 1928 and was widely used during World War II. At the time it was thought it would "retain its sparkling transparency year after year under outdoor conditions." Unfortunately, this proved not to be the case.

To enclose the 40,000-square-foot surface area of the new greenhouse's curved exterior, 4,000 individual pieces of triangular Plexiglas were required, and Synergetics designed 55 different sizes of

ABOVE Glazier Robert Kelly of Nurre Glass Company installing Plexiglas panels with neoprene gaskets on the Climatron, 1960. Of the new material, said Kelly, "It was easier than glass. You could bend it into place."

them to fill the subtly changing spaces between the aluminum geodesic structural elements. These were manufactured by Dayton Plastics, of Dayton, Ohio, and then hung from the aluminum frame. Mackey proposed hanging them with aluminum wire and using neoprene gaskets to seal them within their frames, similar to the curtain wall Eero Saarinen had designed for the General Motors Technical Center in Warren, Michigan, a few years before. This precisely detailed structure was then fabricated by North American Aviation of Columbus, Ohio, which also built other geodesic domes designed by Synergetics. The circular concrete foundation for the aluminum frame was engineered by Stevens, Lopinot and Weber, and then constructed by C. Rallo of St. Louis under

Continued on page 35.

LEFT Interior view of the Climatron, with visitors, 1960s.
RIGHT Synergetics, Inc. (James Fitzgibbon and Pete Barnwell), Climatron original construction documents cover page, 1959.

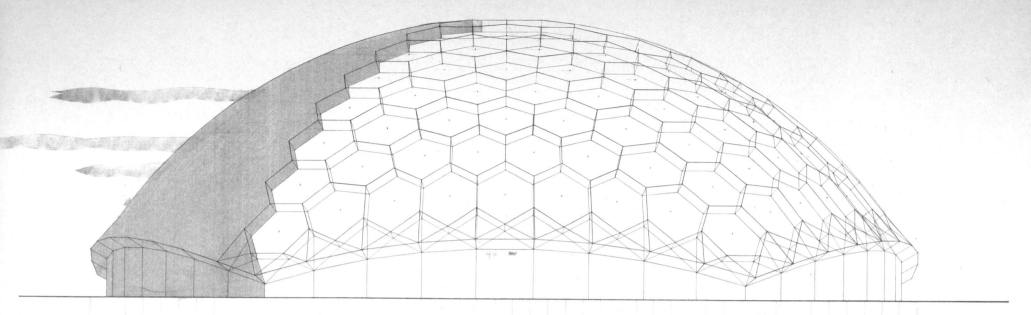

GEODESIC DOME FOR SHAW'S GARDEN — ST. LOUIS, MO.

THESE DRAWINGS ARE FOR DOME FRAME & GUTTER, SKIN, & VENTILATOR   GENERAL PLANNING & WORK BELOW EL. 103'-0" BY MURPHY ~ MACKEY—ARCHITECTS

I N D E X

FRAME ERECTION

E-1   LAYOUT OF SUPPORT POINTS
E-2   PIER (PYLON) & BENT ANCHOR DETAILS
E-3   CURTAIN WALL CONTROL LAYOUT
E-4   DOME FRAME ELEVATION
E-5   DOME FRAME PLAN
E-6   DOME FRAME ELEVATION AT PYLON & DETAILS
E-7   GUTTER INSTALLATION DETAILS
E-8   GUTTER ASSEMBLY LOCATION

FRAME ASSEMBLY

A-1   RADIAL ASSEMBLIES
A-2   COMPRESSION MEMBER ASSEMBLIES
A-3   TENSION VERTEX ASSEMBLY
A-4   BENT & PIER RADIAL ASSEMBLIES
A-5   BENT BRACKET ASSEMBLIES
A-6   GUTTER ASSEMBLIES
A-7   GUTTER CONNECTOR ASSEMBLIES
A-8   GUTTER DOWNSPOUT ASSEMBLY

FRAME PARTS

P-1   TENSION & COMPRESSION RADIAL FITTINGS (CASTINGS)
P-2   RADIAL EXTRUSIONS & BENT ATTACHMENTS
P-3   TUBE & ROD FITTINGS
P-4   COMPRESSION MEMBERS
P-5   TENSION MEMBERS
P-6   BENTS
P-7   GUTTER SECTIONS
P-8   GUTTER PARTS
P-9   GUTTER FITTINGS

SKIN ERECTION

SE-1   PLAN & DETAILS OF SUSPENDED SKIN
SE-2   SKIN FRAME SUSPENSION ASSEMBLIES (FIELD ASSEMBLED)
SE-3   ZENITH VENTILATOR FLASHING ERECTION

SKIN ASSEMBLY

SA-1   SUSPENDED SKIN VERTEX HARDWARE ASSEMBLIES
SA-2   ASSEMBLY OF SKIN TO GUTTER VERTEX CLIPS

SKIN PARTS

SR1   PLEXIGLASS PANELS
SR2   GASKET LOOPS
SR3   SUSPENDED SKIN FRAMING RIBS
SP4   VERTEX PANS, BASE CLIPS, & MISC. HARDWARE
SP5   GUTTER BOUNDARY VERTEX PANS
SP4   ZENITH VENTILATOR FLASHING PARTS
SP-7   ZENITH VENTILATOR FLASHING PARTS

VENTILATOR ERECTION

VE-1   ZENITH VENTILATOR ERECTION

VENTILATOR ASSEMBLY

VA-1   ZENITH VENTILATOR ASSEMBLY

VENTILATOR PARTS

VP-1   ZENITH VENTILATOR PARTS

REFERS TO EACH OF THE 5 BUTTRESSES AT

ELEVATION OF AREA BELOW EDGE TRUSS
AB FROM PENTAGON POINT TO PENTAGON POINT

REVISIONS:	DATE	REVISIONS:	DATE

SYNERGETICS, INC.
3013 HILLSBORO • RALEIGH, N. C.

DATE	ELEVATION & INDEX	CONTRACT	SHEET
APRIL 28, 1959			
SCALE			
1/8" = 1'-0"	SHAWS GARDENS ST. LOUIS		S-26 TITL
DRWN.	GEODESIC DOME		

ENGINEERING FOR THE FUTURE

SYNERGETICS, INC. was the engineering design firm of the Climatron. The firm was founded in 1954 by Buckminster Fuller and James Fitzgibbon in Raleigh, North Carolina. Synergetics firm associate J. Forrest (Pete) Barnwell also had a major role in the firm's design and detailing of the Climatron.

Synergetics designed and built geodesic domes around the world for an impressive array of clients, including the U.S. Marines, Navy, Information Agency, and Department of Commerce. The first trade agency dome was assembled in one day in 1956 in Kabul, Afghanistan; it was 100 feet in diameter and made from aluminum and suspended fabric. It was followed by others in Poznán, Poland; Casablanca, Morocco; Tunis; Istanbul; Delhi, Bombay (Mumbai), and Madras (Chennai), India; Bangkok; Tokyo and Osaka; and Salonika,

9,000 SQUARE FOOT PAVILION   AIR CARGOED   RALEIGH N.C. TO   AFGHANISTAN

A promotional flyer for the Synergetics Kabul dome for the U.S. Trade Agency, 1956.

Greece. Synergetics designed an openwork metal geodesic dome for the American Society of Metals near Cleveland, Ohio (see page 28), and enclosed pavilions at the World's Fairs in Seattle (1961) and

New York (1964). They also designed two large railcar repair facility projects using solid geodesic domes for the Union Tank Car Company in Wood River, Illinois, and Baton Rouge, Louisiana.

Synergetics co-founder James Walter Fitzgibbon (1915–85) was trained in architecture at Syracuse University and the University of Pennsylvania. He taught at the University of Oklahoma before moving with other Oklahoma faculty and students to Raleigh, where they established what is now the College of Design at North Carolina State University. Two of these students, T. C. Howard and Pete Barnwell, later became Fitzgibbon's business partners in Synergetics, Inc.

Buckminster Fuller was also teaching then in Raleigh, and in 1949 he hired Fitzgibbon as head of the Fuller Research Foundation there. Fitzgibbon eventually became Fuller's business partner in three companies, Skybreak Carolina Corporation, Geodesics, Inc., and Synergetics, Inc. As Fuller's worldwide career took off, he sold Synergetics in 1957 to Fitzgibbon, Howard, and Barnwell, who continued the Raleigh-based firm. In 1968, Synergetics seems to have ceased operations and Fitzgibbon joined the faculty of the School of Architecture of Washington University in St. Louis, where he had previously taught as a visitor, sometimes with Fuller.

"SPECIALISTS IN THE DESIGN AND DEVELOPMENT OF LIGHT-WEIGHT, MODULAR, PREFABRICATED, AND GEODESIC STRUCTURES."

Continued from page 30.

the supervision of the architects.

After Mackey, Fitzgibbon, and city code officials had finalized the details with North American Aviation in Columbus, a necessary step in obtaining city public safety approvals for such a radical building, construction progressed rapidly by the fall of 1959. Went noted in his diary that "gradually I am realizing what a remarkable structure this is going to be, something utterly different in beauty, size, operation, and botanical possibilities."

As the Climatron construction and fund-raising efforts progressed, the Garden made public Murphy and Mackey's ambitious new 1961 master plan. Very little had been built in the Garden since the Palm House, and now under Went's leadership a whole series

LEFT Detail of the geodesic dome of the Climatron under construction, 1959. **ABOVE** Hexagonal section of the Climatron frame being moved to the site by the contractor, North American Aviation, 1959.

**ABOVE Murphy & Mackey, presentation rendering of
the Climatron, 1959** (by Schell Lewis, New York City).

of new buildings and landscape designs were suggested. The plan proposed the idea of reorganizing the Garden into "regional planting zones," one for each continent, while still retaining the historic areas around Tower Grove House. It also called for a new research building at the north end (where the Ridgway Visitor Center by HOK was later built in 1982), along with restaurants, offices, display areas, and a symphony hall auditorium, all with extensive new parking at the north end of the grounds. This plan reflected Went's vision that the Garden could become a public cultural center for the region, drawing together various activities into what he intended to become more publicly accessible grounds. To help defray the costs of these plans and make the Garden self-supporting, Went also introduced a 50-cent admission fee to the Climatron.

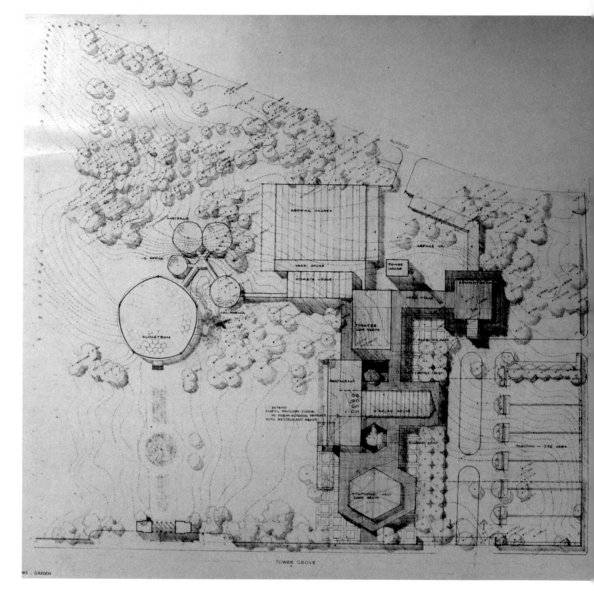

ABOVE Murphy & Mackey, Missouri Botanical Garden master plan, 1961, with proposed concert hall and restaurant. The Climatron was one of several geodesic domes proposed for the Garden by Went for plant research, along with other public facilities, including the first provision at the Garden for visitor parking along Shaw Boulevard.

These plans took place as St. Louis itself was undergoing major transformations. The St. Louis County suburbs were then growing rapidly, attracting the city's middle classes and eventually many of its corporate offices as well. Both partners of Murphy and Mackey had designed houses for themselves, in University City (1939) and Ladue (1948), respectively, when those areas were still near the western edge of metropolitan development. Saarinen's Arch design downtown, the winner of a 1947 competition, finally went into construction in 1958, after Mackey, as president of the local American Institute of Architects chapter, played an important role in orchestrating civic support and then obtaining the necessary federal funding for it to proceed. The interstate highway system was also taking shape, changing the transportation patterns of the region and helping to pull business and residents out of the city toward the metropolitan periphery, which began to surround a much larger urbanized area. One of the first modern airports in the world was built in St. Louis, the predecessor to Eero Saarinen's TWA Terminal at Kennedy Airport in New York. Yamasaki's Lambert

Field Main Terminal featured some of the first thin-shell concrete vault structures in America and marked the point when concrete structural innovations began to enter the architectural mainstream.

This was also the era of "slum clearance" urban renewal in the city, and large areas on all sides of the downtown were demolished (as the Old Waterfront already had been in 1939), for various public housing and industrial renewal projects. The 1960 master plan for downtown itself called for building a series of large parking garages directly connected to the new interstate highway (I-64/US-40) then under construction. It was thought that these massive garages, modeled after similar unbuilt projects by Louis Kahn for Center City Philadelphia and by Victor Gruen for downtown Fort Worth, would allow visitors to drive, park, and then

ABOVE Aerial view of the Mid-America Jubilee, September 1, 1956. Following "slum clearance," the St. Louis riverfront stood empty for nearly two decades while awaiting the construction of the Jefferson National Expansion Memorial. This fair was designed to "dramatize the many assets and attributes that make metropolitan St. Louis such an outstanding community in which to live and work." At center is a Fuller-designed geodesic dome billed as "the latest word in engineering and technology." It housed the "World of Fashion" in an era when St. Louis was still "first in shoes" and junior miss clothing.

walk to their destinations within a "pedestrianized" new urban core. As part of the plan, most of the entire area south of Market Street was cleared, and construction would soon commence on a new home for the Cardinals, the first Busch Stadium (1966–2007). Ultimately, most of these urban renewal activities damaged the declining city more than simple neglect. Nonetheless, these massive reconstruction activities were the background to the renewal of the Garden and to the construction of the Climatron, which proved to be an immense popular success.

Went had considered other names for the new structure, including "plantosphere," "sylvarium," and "floradome," but decided that "climatron," with its Greek last syllable meaning a large machine, was the best choice for what he envisioned to be mainly a scientific laboratory to study plant growth. He planned the 24,000 square feet of area to be subdivided into four district climate zones, with the two in the eastern half to be built eleven feet higher than the two in the western half, the result of reusing the foundations of the Palm House and some of its plantings. An "Amazonian forest" was intended for the hottest area, located at the southeast corner. At the south edge, a pond was built with an "aquatunnel," a clear Plexiglas-enclosed tube beneath the water, through which visitors could view aquatic plants from

Continued on page 44.

ABOVE The aquatunnel, an enclosed six-foot-high Plexiglas pedestrian tube in the original Climatron interior. It was submerged in the pond at the south end, so that visitors could view aquatic plants. It was removed in the 1988–90 renovations.

MID-CENTURY MODERN IN ST. LOUIS

by Esley Hamilton, St. Louis County Parks Historian

What we call "modern" architecture was revolutionary when it emerged in Europe in the years around World War I. It rejected the popular historical styles of the time, in fact, the whole idea of styles, replacing them with a design approach based on current needs, materials, and technology. The first example in the St. Louis region was Harris Armstrong's 1935 medical building for Leo Shanley, which received national attention.

Armstrong was followed by other daring architects in the years leading up to World War II, including Isadore Shank, Edouard Mutrux, William Bernoudy, Charles Eames, Frederick Dunn, Charles Nagel, Joseph Murphy, Eugene Mackey, Jr., Gyo Obata, and Kenneth Wischmeyer. After the war, modernism was embraced by the younger generation of architects, and it found enthusiastic patrons, not only private residential clients, but major public institutions. Religious groups in this region became national leaders in adopting modern architecture.

Shanley Orthodontic Clinic, Harris Armstrong, 1935.

Abbey Chapel at the St. Louis Priory, HOK, 1962.

scorned achievements of the Victorian era are again admired, so eventually will be the best of the modern movement. That trend has already begun, especially among young people. But running counter to that trend is the increasingly frequent demolition of buildings from this era. At this rate, will anything be left? While Victorian row houses were built by the hundreds, the best modern buildings, particularly the institutional ones, were one of a kind. Once they are gone, they are gone forever.

The acceptance of modern design began to wane in the 1970s, and by now the achievements of the modern movement dating from the 1930s through the 1960s seem more alien to many observers than the Victorian works they reacted against, a historic reversal of fashion. We know from history, however, that taste is cyclical. Just as the once-

ST. LOUIS MOD HIGHLIGHTS

SHANLEY ORTHODONTIC CLINIC 1935
ARCHITECT: Harris Armstrong

GATEWAY ARCH 1965
ARCHITECT: Eero Saarinen

KRAUS HOUSE (*now the Frank Lloyd Wright House in Ebsworth Park*) 1955
ARCHITECT: Frank Lloyd Wright

LAMBERT FIELD MAIN TERMINAL 1955
ARCHITECTS: Hellmuth, Yamasaki, & Leinweber

THE ABBEY CHAPEL, ST. LOUIS PRIORY 1962
ARCHITECTS: Hellmuth, Obata & Kassabaum

B'NAI AMOONA SYNAGOGUE (*now COCA*) 1950
ARCHITECT: Eric Mendelsohn

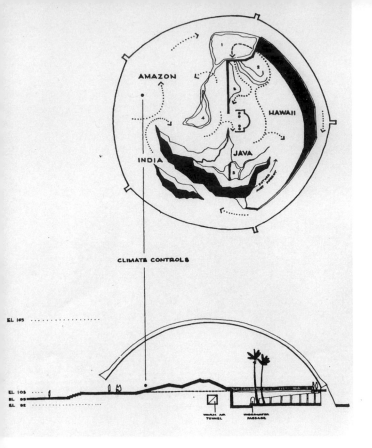

Continued from page 41.

below. At the southwest corner was to be the oceanic climate of "Little Hawaii," with artificially created cool days and warm nights, containing rice paddies, tropical flowers, and fruit trees. At the northwest corner, there was to be a "Javanese mountain mist forest," with a waterfall and a pool filled with floating volcanic pumice boulders. Here both days and nights would be cool. Finally, at the northeast corner was to be an Indian mountain and stream environment, with figs, avocados, and other fruit-bearing plants. Adjacent to it were ferns and cycads from the Palm House, some of which still grow there. In the center, between the eastern and western halves, was a staircase topped with classical columns from the demolished Palm House.

The Climatron's official opening on October 1, 1960 drew 2,000 to 3,500 people, and the building was hailed as an "eighth wonder of the world" by the media. The structure was lit with 1000-watt incandescent bulbs, providing a dramatic nighttime vision at its inception. Nothing else like it then existed, as the first geodesic dome greenhouse. The president of the National Academy of Science, Dr. Detlev Bronk, then also president of Rockefeller University in New York, gave the opening speech, "Science, Man, and Nature." This was followed by remarks by St. Louis Mayor Raymond Tucker, Washington University Chancellor Ethan Shepley, the

TOP Murphy & Mackey, Plan and section of the Climatron, showing the original four climate zones planned for it (*American Institute of Architects Journal*, May 1961). **BOTTOM** View of the columns from the Palm House at the center of the Climatron before renovation in 1990. **RIGHT The Climatron at night reflected in tropical lily pool, 1960.**

director of the New York Botanic Garden, and others. In the first month after the opening the number of visitors to the Garden for the first time exceeded the 1928 total, and, aided by an immense wave of national and local publicity, the Climatron was well on its way to becoming an icon.

In 1961, Murphy and Mackey were awarded the R. S. Reynolds Memorial Award for its design, a $25,000 prize from the American Institute of Architects for a work in which "aluminum has been an important contributing factor." The design jury, chaired by Minoru Yamasaki, the Detroit-area architect of the World Trade Center and many other buildings including the Lambert Airport main terminal, hailed the "tropical lyricism of

RIGHT Reynolds award presentation, 1961. Climatron design architects Eugene J. Mackey, Jr. (center) and his partner Joseph Murphy (right) receiving the R. J. Reynolds Memorial Award for "a significant work of architecture, in the creation of which aluminum has been an important contributing factor."

the botanical displays" within the umbrella-like structure that created a "shadowless" interior. Mackey rather unusually chose to share the large amount of the award with all the members of the design team.

Yet despite this very positive popular and professional response, the Climatron had few imitators. Although Synergetics and Fuller himself continued to design geodesic domes for various purposes, very few other such greenhouse structures were constructed. Similar in some ways to the Climatron in its geodesic dome design, Fuller's science pavilion for the 1964 New York's World's Fair, reopened in 1968 as the Queens Zoo Aviary, is not a greenhouse. Nor really is Fuller and Shoji Sadao's U.S. Pavilion at the Montreal Expo '67, commissioned by the U.S. Information Agency in 1964. Fuller saw the Expo '67 dome—a 250-foot diameter sphere constructed of welded steel trusses (which Fuller and Fitzgibbon called "octet")—as the next step beyond the Climatron. Fuller designed its exterior like an

TOP Original entrance of the Climatron. Visitors inserted a token worth 50 cents into a turnstyle to enter. **BOTTOM Buckminster Fuller and Shoji Sadao, United States Pavilion, Expo '67, Montreal, Canada, 1965.**

animate skin, one that could "breathe" through exhaust vents and which would automatically respond to sunlight with 4,700 triangular computer-controlled solar-powered metalized plastic sunshades on cables that would open and close with the sun's daily cycle. This proved difficult technically, and Fuller's associated firm of Geodesics, working here again with Paul Londe as the mechanical engineer, was not completely successful in solving all the problems involved in the design. Inadequate lubrication caused many of the solar cell motors to freeze up after completion, and left many of the shades permanently open. In 1975 a fire destroyed most of the structure, which nonetheless had attracted much favorable comment at the exhibition.

By the mid-1960s Fuller had become a design guru to a new generation of students and designers, but he never actually built in St. Louis, despite his many professional ties to the area. His only built works nearby are the Union Tank Car railway repair facility nearby in Wood River, Illinois (1959), designed with the same engineering team as the Climatron, and his own dome house in Carbondale, Illinois. He is often still remembered locally, however, for his "Old Man River" project to put a one-mile-diameter dome over a large, energy-efficient, high-density, mixed-use complex in East St. Louis. Commissioned in 1970 by choreographer and dancer Katherine Dunham to help revive the troubled industrial city, the dome

ABOVE Synergetics, Inc. (James Fitzgibbon and Pete Barnwell), Union Tank Car railway car repair facility, Wood River, Illinois, 2009.

was to be sited along the Mississippi River just north of the
Martin Luther King, Jr., Bridge, and would house some 125,000
people, along with commercial and industrial space. (See page
27.) Fuller thought the construction of the project would create
thousands of jobs, and efforts to build it had a certain amount
of political support as late as the early 1990s, when it began to
seem improbably utopian for such a devastated area.

The structures that come closest to the Climatron in both
design and purpose are the recent Desert Dome (2002) at the
Henry Doorly Zoo in Omaha, a 230-foot diameter geodesic dome with acrylic panels which encloses
what is said to be the world's largest indoor desert, and the Eden Project in Cornwall, England, opened
in 2001, which uses multiple geodesic domes to present a variety of ecosystems. A visual parallel to the
Climatron is the Mitchell Park Conservatory in Milwaukee, Wisconsin, but these tall glass structures from
the 1950s are not geodesic domes, but rather beehives in structure.

TOP **MERO, Eden Project biomes, near St. Austell, Cornwall, England, 2001**. Built in an abandoned clay
quarry, these geodesic domes comprise the world's largest greenhouse and are constructed of tubular steel
space frames clad with a thermoplastic called EFTE. At right is architect Nicholas Grimshaw's Eden Project
Core building, 2006. BOTTOM **Desert Dome at the Henry Doorly Zoo, Omaha, Nebraska, 2002**. A 230-foot
diameter geodesic dome with acrylic panels that encloses what is said to be the world's largest indoor desert.

The reasons why the Climatron itself does not seem to have been widely imitated soon became evident. The elaborate climatic control system using fans and water sprays, centered in a Honeywell computer called the Supervisory Data Center, never functioned well, and it was able to produce only two rather than the four complex climatic zones intended. This made the structure more suitable as a simple tropical greenhouse than the research facility Went had envisioned. At the same time, its supposedly long-lasting Plexiglas panels began to discolor after a few years, making steady light conditions for plant growth unpredictable. Yet even so, the structure with its distinctive aluminum geodesic frame remained immensely popular, as it still is today. The Climatron's old interior, with its "aquatunnel" and two-level designs, is now fondly remembered by generations of St. Louisans, and anecdotes about the Climatron have become part of St. Louis urban lore.

ABOVE Donald Grieb, Mitchell Park Conservatory domes, Milwaukee, 1959–67. These three beehive-shaped glass domes are not geodesic domes, but their function is similar to that of the Climatron. They are called the Arid, Tropical, and Floral Show domes, and are each 140 feet in diameter and 85 feet high.

Went himself, however, soon departed from the Garden. He came into conflict with the Board of Trustees and resigned in 1963, eventually accepting the directorship at the Desert Research Institute of the University of Nevada—Reno in 1965. His vision for the Garden did not come to pass as he intended, and the additional Climatron-like domes he planned to link to the first one for additional research experiments were not built. In the years immediately after his departure, the Garden Board President declared that the Garden would return to "preserving old traditions." These included the construction of new lily ponds in front of the Climatron in 1964. They did not carry out Went's ambitious agenda of making the Garden a popular attraction with a symphony hall and other public uses.

The idea of the Garden as a public gathering place was instead brought to fruition in a quite different way over a decade later, under Dr. Peter H. Raven's directorship, which began in 1971. Raven hoped to bring in English landscape designer John Symonds to expand the public areas and make them

ABOVE The Climatron Supervisory Data Center, which used a Honeywell computer to control air movement, artificial light, and temperature. Underground electric cables and compressed-air lines linked it to lights, large fans, and air sprays. At the center was a continuous temperature record that used a stylographic pen to record the readings of the ten temperature stations in the original Climatron, which were hidden beneath vegetation.

more ecologically diverse. Ultimately he commissioned the Pittsburgh firm of Environmental Planning and Design (EPD), now known as MTR, to give form to these concepts. Like Went, Raven also sought to make more of the Garden's grounds open to the public. He greatly admired the innovative Climatron and the ideas behind it, but did not want it to dominate the

ABOVE The Screw pine (*Pandanus utilis*) during the Climatron renovation construction, around 1990. At center is Garden Director Dr. Peter H. Raven.

surroundings. Instead, he and EPD embarked on a long series of improvements that have given the Garden much of its current form.

As those changes were beginning, the Climatron and its architects were appropriately honored at the structure's twentieth anniversary. By 1988, there was no question that the geodesic greenhouse structure had to remain, yet it became apparent that renovations were necessary. At that point, its clouded Plexiglas surface had been in use for 28 years, and an engineering report commissioned from EPD indicated that the original aluminum frame had become unsafe. A new steel superstructure was built within, supporting an entirely new glass skin. The Plexiglas was replaced with Saflex, laminated glass panels with an interlayer, similar to what is used in automobile windshields. Its detailing, which can be seen under the now non-functional aluminum frame, is quite different from the original design. The foundations and the steel frame bents from the original design are also still in place. Although it was possible to retain many of the existing plants in place during the renovation, including cycads which had also been in the Palm House, the

ABOVE The original Plexiglas sheathing of the Climatron was only supposed to be in place for a few years. Instead, it was maintained for nearly 30 years, becoming progressively more scratched and opaque as seen here during its removal.

Climatron's layout was completely changed in the renovation. Its entrances were redesigned and the two distinct ground levels splitting the structure at the staircase at the center were modified to create a more sloping topography along a meandering path that winds under the new glass inner dome. The large wooden classical columns and stone stairs from the Palm House that had been a prominent feature at the center of the Climatron's original interior were removed, as the columns had deteriorated and the stairs were not wheelchair-accessible. The focus of the renovation was to increase biodiversity while retaining the attractive tropical look, and to that end, new features like the waterfall in the southeast corner and the rustic bridge in the northwest corner were added. New and much better mechanical and lighting systems were also installed. The renovated Climatron reopened on March 30, 1990, and many additional years of use for it were secured.

ABOVE During Climatron renovations in the late 1980s, the aluminum geodesic frame of the original Climatron was kept, but its discolored Plexiglas panels were removed and a new steel and glass structure was built beneath it. The new structure was glazed with Saflex laminated glass panels, similar to the material used in automobile windshields.

Since then, the Climatron's iconic significance has not diminished. For many visitors, it is still the most intriguing structure in the Garden, and one that seems to best embody the Garden's international mission of research and conservation around the world. The contrast between the familiar Midwestern seasons of the Garden grounds outside and the lush tropical atmosphere of the Climatron's interior,

ABOVE View of renovated Climatron interior, 1990, designed by EPD (now MTR) of Pittsburgh, Pennsylvania.

with its dramatic waterfall and wide range of exotic plants, remains memorable and draws enthusiasts year after year, season after season. Far fewer visitors probably notice the architectural and structural aspects of this innovative building, which first gave Went's and Fuller's ideas permanent form in a somewhat improbable setting at the time: a shabby, genteel old institution in a declining part of the city.

Today, of course, geodesic dome greenhouses are commonplace, and ones like the Plexiglas butterfly dome in the St. Louis Zoo insectarium are an almost inevitable feature in spaces for ecological education. It takes considerable mental effort now to imagine what the impact must have been of Fuller's futuristic ideas in the dowdy Garden of 1960, and to re-experience the sense of a new and technologically driven future that the Climatron must have then inspired. That future as it was then understood, of course, soon proved to be far from unproblematic, and we are still struggling to make sense of the complex legacies of that perhaps overly optimistic era. It is rare that a building from that time is still valued for its original futuristic vision and innovative exposed technology. The Climatron's 50th anniversary as a St. Louis icon is indeed something to celebrate. ✿

LEFT A reception during the Garden's annual botanical Systematics Symposium in 1990, the year of the grand re-opening of the Climatron.

CLIMATRON: A PORTRAIT

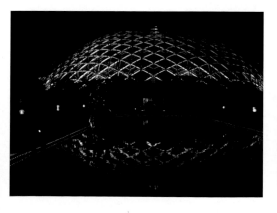

DAY

The day unfolds like

a lotus bloom,

Pink at the tip and

gold at the core,

Rising up swiftly through

waters of gloom

That lave night's shore.

–Mary McNeil Fenellosa

KALEIDOSCOPE OF COLORS:
Each year, staff horticulturists design a fresh look for the beds surrounding the Climatron. Springtime brings ruffled double tulips and tall black 'Queen of the Night' tulips one year, two-tone *Narcissus* the next. A candy-colored assortment is selected to mirror the floating *Walla Walla* sculptures by Dale Chihuly. Silhouettes of palms and trees appear as the sun sets in the west.

IN LOVING MEMORY
OF 1ST LT. FREDERICK W. DUNLAP 135TH AAF WW II
BY HIS DEVOTED BROTHER EUGENE W. DUNLAP

A TREASURED MEMORY: Thousands of school children visit the Climatron each year. Under the waterfall, this indoor rain forest is home to over 2,300 tropical plants. Visitors can learn about many helpful economic plant species, such as the banyan used in traditional medicine to treat diabetes. Five full-time staff and eight volunteers keep this half-acre jungle from growing unchecked.

NIGHT

Evening now

unbinds the fetters

Fashioned by the

glowing light;

All that breathe are

thankful debtors

To the harbinger

of night.

–William Wordsworth

A SCULPTURE GARDEN: At night, the Climatron is often lit from within, adding another sculpture to the landscape. The pools showcase works by Swedish artist Carl Milles, including the three *Angel Musicians* on their pedestals and farther west, *Two Girls Dancing* (above). During the warmer months, the floating blown-glass *Walla Wallas, 2006* by Dale Chihuly join the scene.

EARLY MORN TIL DAWN: The *Orpheus Fountain Figures* by Carl Milles frame a misty view of the lit Climatron at midnight. Even when dark, the Climatron has a dramatic presence in the landscape, evoking by turns a mound from the prehistoric mound-builders of the region, a solar eclipse, and a futuristic spaceship.

SEASONS

I hail the seasons

as they go,

I woo the sunshine,

brave the wind.

I scan the lily

and the rose,

I nod to every

nodding tree.

–Elizabeth Stoddard

SLEIGHBELLS RING: Snow turns the landscape into a black-and-white picture, highlighting the Climatron's enduring architectural appeal. While we celebrate the holiday season with hats, gloves, and forced-air heat, inside the Climatron, it's still 85 degrees by day with the warm humidity of Hilo, Hawaii (85 percent). Ahh….

SPRINGTIME FOLLIES: Spring comes early inside the Climatron, with a rush of blooming orchids in January and February. Outside, the Climatron is the backdrop to the Egg-stravaganza egg hunt for children of Garden members. Blooming magnolias, azaleas, and eventually tulips line the path approaching this historic conservatory.

SUMMERTIME FUNTIME:
During the dog days of summer in St. Louis when the mercury climbs into the triple digits, the Climatron is surprisingly refreshing by comparison at only 85 degrees. The central reflecting pools are a riot of color as the Garden's renowned collection of tropical water lilies burst into bloom, framing the most famous view of the Climatron.

SONG OF AUTUMN: The Climatron is seen through the shifting colors of the deciduous bald cypress of the central axis; through the Missouri hardwoods of the Rhodendron Garden; and fringed by golden ginkgos planted by Garden founder Henry Shaw himself. It's fun to imagine what Shaw would have thought of this futuristic greenhouse!

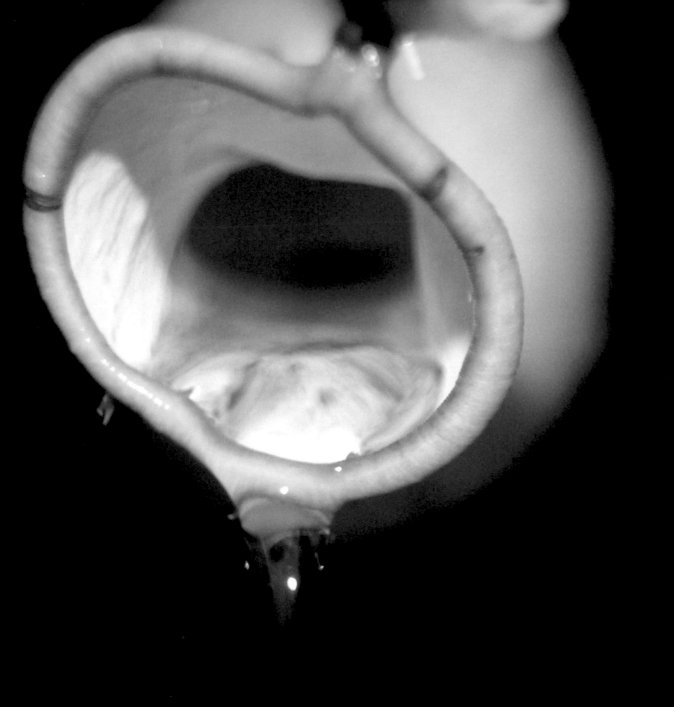

PLANTS, ANIMALS, & ART

The experience is immersion, sensory abandon, submission to an almost primeval overload of plants, smells, and humidity… a fantasy of what nature might once have been, a sensual engulfment…

–Robert Riley, Harvard Design Magazine, *on visiting the Climatron.*

TROPICAL CARNIVORE: *Nepenthes* traps and drowns insects in the pitcher-shaped parts of their leaves.

GLASS UNDER GLASS: *Sunset Herons, 2003* by Dale Chihuly rises from a display of aquatic plants.

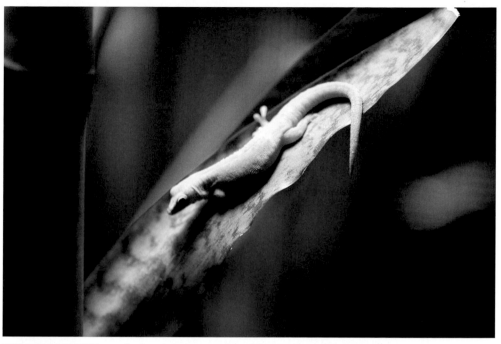

ECO-PEST CONTROL: gecko lizards help control the Climatron insect population.

TROPICAL SOUNDTRACK: the blue-gray tanager is one of many songbirds in the Climatron.

MOST DIVERSE ECOSYSTEM ON EARTH: The tropics are home to an estimated 160,000 of the earth's 300,000 plant species. Inside the Climatron, visitors can marvel at prehistoric cycads and their egg-like blooms. Houseplants that grow to monstrous sizes with leaves spanning a foot and vines as thick as your arm. Unusual green-blooming flowers, such as the blue jade vine (*Strongylodon macrobotrys*), native to the Philippines. Plant co-evolvers like fungi, insects, even birds. And dozens of economic plants, such as rice, pineapple, and banana.

THE NUMBERS BEHIND THE SHAPES

In mathematics, geodesics (Greek geo *"earth" +* daiein *"divide") are paths that travel the shortest distance between two points. While we often think of the shortest distance between two points as a straight line, this is not true for the surface of a sphere. The shortest path between two points on a surface of a sphere lies along a "great circle," that is, a circle that divides the sphere into two equal halves, such as the lines of longitude on the globe.*

GEOMETRY

To build a geodesic dome you would start with a polyhedron, usually an icosahedron. An icosahedron (Greek *eikosi* "twenty" + *hedron* "face") has 20 triangular faces.

Unlike the Epcot Center at Walt Disney World which is fully spherical, you will actually only need half (or less than half) of your icosahedron to make a dome.

Subdivide each triangle into more triangles. The number of times you subdivide a side of your triangle is called the **frequency** of the dome. For example, this figure (at lower left) has a frequency of 4. Can you determine the frequency of the Climatron dome? The higher the frequency, the more triangles there are—and the stronger the dome will be.

Notice that most of the points (or **vertices**) of the subdivided triangle are surrounded by six triangular faces making a hexagon. The triangles are equilateral, so each angle is 60 degrees. Thus, each vertex of the hexagon has a total angle of 360 degrees (6 x 60).

These small triangles are all the same size, but they do not lie on the surface of a sphere. Instead, they lie on the flat faces of the icasohedron inside a sphere. Imagine drawing your triangles on the surface of a deflated

Icosahedron

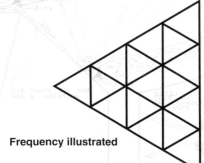

Frequency illustrated

ABOVE Spaceship Earth at the Epcot Center, Walt Disney World, is a geodesic sphere.

balloon and then blowing it up until it filled the sphere. Now you have the design for your geodesic dome. One of the major construction challenges of geodesic domes is that this projection process—blowing your balloon to fill the sphere–distorts the lengths and the triangles are now all slightly different sizes—an engineering nightmare.

Back to our 360-degree hexagons. They exist on the flat figure. We have to bend it down to form the half-sphere, and thus, some vertices have to be less than 360 degrees. To make a spherical figure, we need to have an angular deficit of 360 degrees—or 6 vertices with only five triangles instead of the usual six. Instead of hexagons, we need a few **pentagons**.

Look at the photos at right. Can you spot one pentagon visible on the Climatron in this photo? How about in this geodesic-dome jungle gym from nearby Tower Grove Park?

TOP Aerial view of the Climatron, 2009, showing one prominent pentagon among hexagons. **BOTTOM** Geodesic jungle gym in Tower Grove Park, 2009, also with pentagon visible.

A LOWLAND RAIN FOREST UNDER GLASS

The tropics are an evolutionary powerhouse—the most diverse ecosystem on the planet. Tropical plants account for 160,000 of the earth's estimated 350,000 species of plants. No building could begin to house all of the diverse plant forms found in the tropics, but the Climatron offers an introduction.

Tropical lowland rain forests lie between the Tropic of Cancer and the Tropic of Capricorn, or 1,400 miles north and south of the Equator. They receive regularly distributed rainfall throughout the year and remain constantly frost free and warm (70–85°F). Inside the Climatron, a computerized climate control system imitates these conditions, maintaining a temperature range from 64°F (29°C) at night to a high of 85°F (18°C) during the day. The average humidity is 85 percent. Plants are watered daily by hand with purified, tempered water similar to rain water.

CLIMATRON STAFF James Cocos, *Vice President of Horticulture*; Deborah Lalumondier, *Senior Horticulturist;* Tutti Gomillia; Melissa Ecker; Michelle Gray; Susie Ratcliff
CLIMATRON VOLUNTEERS Barbara Anderson, Susan Butler, Cari Curtis, Patrick Driscoll, Gene Jarvis, Polly Kinslowe, Tamara Pisoni, Warren Tabachik, Andrew Tonner

About half of the plants in the Climatron were collected in the field, which gives them more scientific value than plants raised in a greenhouse. The Climatron is also home to representatives of numerous endangered species. Just preserving single specimens of endangered plants cannot save a species. However, the Missouri Botanical Garden hopes that once you view these amazing plants, you'll join us in our goal to preserve the biodiversity of the rain forest for future generations.

SPECIAL PLANTS & ANIMALS

Tropical plants provide us with many of our most important foods, and visitors to the Climatron can see the plants that provide sugar, coffee, chocolate, vanilla, bananas, and other common—and not so common—fruits, all in a natural setting.

Other highlights of the collection include the cycads, primitive relatives of conifers dating to the age of the dinosaurs. Some of the Climatron cycads were exhibited at the 1904 World's Fair and are close to 200 years old. The double coconut is an endangered species and very rare in cultivation. It generates the largest seeds in the entire plant kingdom. Epiphytes are plants that grow perched on other plants, taking their sustenance from air and rain. Unusual orchids, aroids, and ferns are just some of the epiphytes found in the Climatron.

The Climatron is also home to many fascinating creatures. Colorful fish swim in the Amazonian aquarium. Look for birds including the blue-grey tanager, green-winged dove, and saffron finch, among others. View poison dart frogs up-close in the nearby Brookings Interpretive Center.

PLANTS AS MEDICINE

Many traditional medicines are made from tropical plants. Tropical plants account for nearly half of all plant species on Earth. Less than 1 percent have been scientifically tested for medical applications, and yet 25 percent of our prescription medicines derive from this tiny portion of tested plants. To learn more, take the Climatron Medicinal Plant tour available in person or online at www.climatron.org.

Medicinal Plant

A Super-Tree

Kapok can be over 200 feet tall! Many people think it is a sacred tree because of its great size. Kapok is a valuable tree in many tropical countries. It provides wood, oil, and food, and the long seed hairs are used for insulation and stuffing.

Kapok bark is used in Nigeria and India to treat diabetes. Chimpanzees also eat kapok flowers and fruit. A group of chimps in Sierra Leone invented stick tools to protect their feet from the young tree's sharp thorns.

Image from the Missouri Botanical Garden rare book collection.

Kapok | *Ceiba pentandra* | Malvaceae, the cotton family | Tropical America and Africa

THE UNSEEN GARDEN

The Climatron conservatory presents the sights, sounds, and smells of a lowland tropical rain forest. It is the popular and public face of behind-the-scenes Garden activities around the globe. Unseen by visitors, the Missouri Botanical Garden operates one of the world's most active research and conservation programs in the tropics.

The tropics do not contain the largest plants, or even necessarily the most unusual plants, but they do contain a greater number of different kinds of plants than all the other areas of the world put together. The comparable figures for tropical animals, especially insects, are even greater. Among this great diversity are plants that have medicinal potential that could benefit many people. But a huge percentage of these plants are vanishing before our very eyes, threatened by the explosive growth of human populations, our increasing consumption rates, and the uses of technologies that are often unsustainable.

The Garden's 46 Ph.D.-level botanists are engaged in a race against time

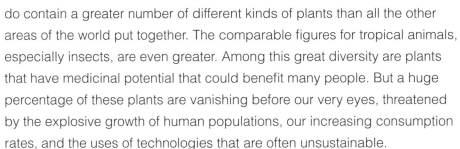

LEFT Dr. Thomas Croat in Ecuador with his 100,000th collection, making him the fourth botanist ever to have collected so many. The plant became the six millionth specimen in the Garden's herbarium, one of the largest and fastest growing research facilities in the world. Herbaria are valuable tools in documenting the characteristics of plants because they allow scientists to compare plants from all over the world side by side. **ABOVE** In Peru, school children in the Yanesha community harvest tomatoes from a school garden. Garden scientists work closely with the local communities of the Palcazú Valley to establish environmental education programs, such as organic community gardens and even a small restaurant (The Honeybee). Through education, local people are inspired to protect their natural resources.

to seek out, document, and classify unknown tropical plants before they become extinct. Under contract with the National Cancer Institute, Garden botanists are also collecting plants that are screened for anti-cancer activity and for pharmaceutical evaluation in programs with other governmental and corporate research groups. Field researchers work with local scientists to strengthen local botanical institutions and train new botanists.

Garden scientists are also involved in innovative community-based conservation programs through the Garden's Center for Conservation and Sustainable Development. One recent example is the creation of a rainforest preserve on the Masoala Peninsula in Madagascar. A unique aspect of this project is that the people who live near the preserve are being taught sustainable agricultural techniques so that they can survive without destroying the forest.

In St. Louis, the Garden's researchers operate out of the Monsanto Center, a state-of-the art model of green architecture and home to the Garden's renowned botanical library and rare book collection. The Garden boasts one of the world's largest herbariums with over 6 million plant specimens, and administers Tropicos, one of the largest natural history databases on the planet.

ABOVE Garden botanists in Vietnam in Yok Don National Park. They collected over 1,000 specimens, but just as importantly trained park rangers in collection and inventory techniques. The Garden collaborates with local institutions around the world to build scientific capacity and knowledge in countries that need it most.

JOIN US
Plants form the basis of human life. Through the extraordinary process of photosynthesis, a small portion of the abundant flow of energy from the sun is converted into the requirements for human existence—food, clothing, shelter, fuel, beauty, medicine, and, over the course of billions of years, oxygen. Thus all life on Earth depends on plants, and we must protect them to save ourselves. Won't you help us by visiting www.mobot.org and becoming a member of the Missouri Botanical Garden today?

CLIMATRON FUN NUMBERS

Diameter: 175 feet—wider than a football field

Volume: 1.3 million cubic feet

Ground surface: 24,000 square feet—or over ½ acre

Cost to build in 1960: $776,000 (or
   $5.6 million in 2009 dollars)

Cost to renovate in 1990: $6 million (or
   $9.8 million in 2009 dollars)

Species represented: 1,400

Percentage of tropical species: 0.9

Panes of Saflex® in today's dome: 2,425

Visitors during the first week: 4,000

Visitors today per year: 757,000

85%
AVERAGE HUMIDITY:
or the average humidity of Hilo, Hawaii

85°F
DAYTIME TEMPERATURE:
or the average temp. of April in Orlando

64°F
NIGHTTIME TEMPERATURE:
or the average temp. of September in San Francisco

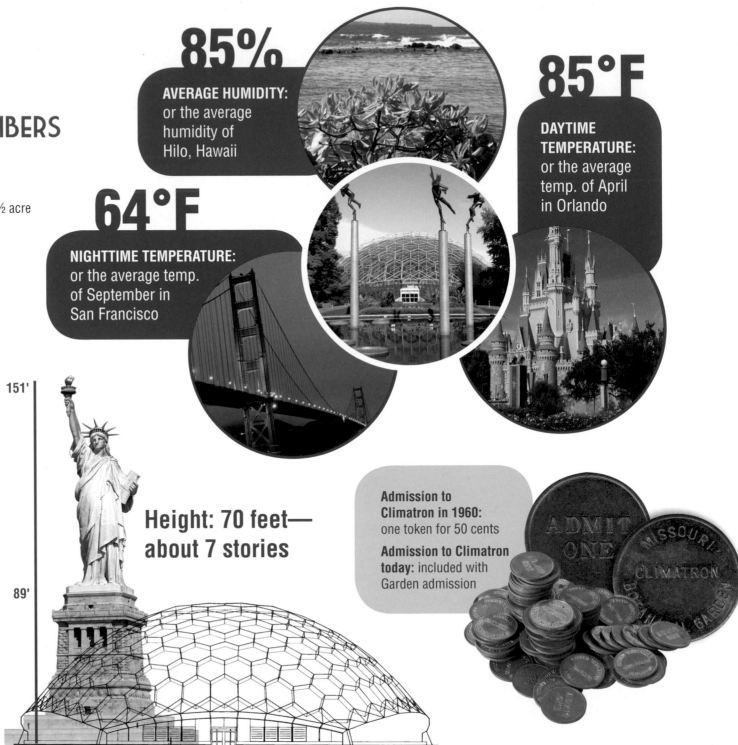

2,233 plants

151'

89'

Height: 70 feet— about 7 stories

Admission to Climatron in 1960: one token for 50 cents

Admission to Climatron today: included with Garden admission

ADMIT ONE

MISSOURI CLIMATRON BOTANICAL GARDEN

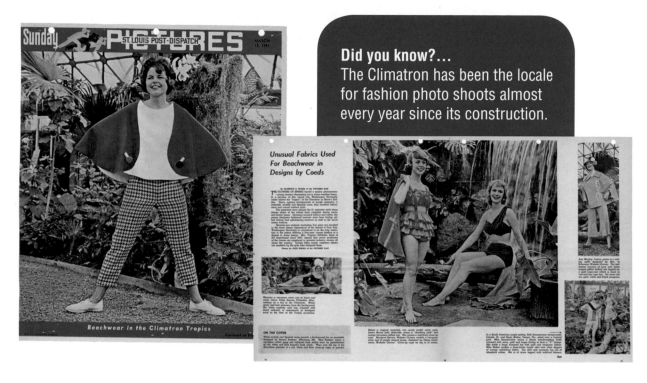

Beachwear in the Climatron Tropics

Did you know?...
The Climatron has been the locale for fashion photo shoots almost every year since its construction.

MAJOR AWARDS

- In **1961**, the architects won the **Reynolds Award for architectural excellence** in a structure using aluminum.

- In **1976**, the Climatron was recognized by a bicentennial commission as one of the **100 most significant architectural achievements in the history of the United States.**

DID YOU KNOW?...

- In the **Cold War era**, tables of the engineering info for geodesic domes were guarded like military secrets.

- **The Climatron was the inspiration** for Douglass Trumbull's 1972 cult classic science fiction film **Silent Running**, starring Bruce Dern.

- **Common houseplants**, such as pothos and philodendron, grow to huge sizes in the Climatron, with leaves almost a foot across.

- The Climatron® was one of the **first major architectural uses** of **Plexiglas**.

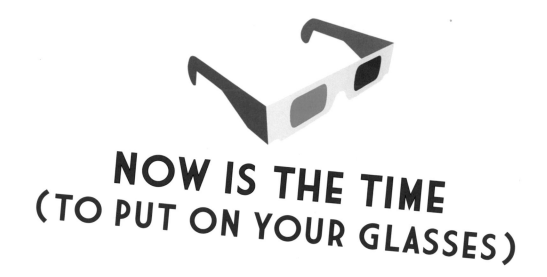

NOW IS THE TIME
(TO PUT ON YOUR GLASSES)

For best results, look at these pictures in bright light!

3-D PHOTOGRAPHY BY DAVID E. KLUTHO

3-D graphics by ron labbe/studio 3D

AN EXPERIENCE OF SENSORY IMMERSION...

>"We water every day by hand for 2 to 4 hours, depending on the season."
– *Deborah Lalumondier, Senior Horticulturist*

^ Cycads date back 300 million years to the time of the dinosaurs.

< Over 100,000 school children visit the Climatron each year.

A TROPICAL GREEN-WINGED DOVE LIVES
IN THE CLIMATRON RAIN FOREST.

< Carnivorous *Nepenthes*
> *Sunset Herons* by Dale Chihuly

THIS CYCAD WAS
DISPLAYED AT THE 1904
WORLD'S FAIR.

3-D EFFECTS

In typical eyesight, the right and the left eye each sees slightly different images (parallax). The brain puts them together to create the complete three-dimensional view of the scene. Printed images in a book are flat (i.e., two-dimensional). The images in the previous 3-D section are called "anaglyph," a 3-D process that combines the left and right eye views when you wear the provided glasses. The red lens hides one image, the cyan lens hides the other, and thus each eye sees a slightly different picture. Your brain is then able to put the views together to show you these photos of the Climatron in amazing 3-D as if you were there.

The earliest 3-D images were created in the mid-19th century. These early stereographs had left and right views next to each other on a single card. A stereoscope viewer (see left) allowed each eye to see only one of the images. With the advent of anaglyph technology, movies in 3-D and 3-D comic books became widely popular in mainstream media in the 1950s, about the same time the Climatron was built. Today, 3-D movies are enjoying a renaissance of popularity. The technology used, however, is not anaglyph but *polarization*, which is more easily viewed with less eye-strain over longer periods of time.

STEREOSCOPE: a stereograph viewer from the 19th century.

STEREOGRAPH: This image of the observatory at the Missouri Botanical Garden, circa 1890, appears 3-D when viewed with a stereoscope.

ANAGLYPH:
The same stereograph made into an anaglyph. Look at it with your 3-D glasses.

THE PHOTOGRAPHER
St. Louis-based photographer David E. Klutho shoots professionally for *Sports Illustrated* and is the author of *In Your Face 3-D: the Best 3-D Book Ever!* He used five different 3-D camera rigs to create these fantastic images of the Climatron conservatory and the tropical rain forest inside. He is a member of the National Stereoscopic Association, the New York Stereoscopic Society, and the International Stereoscopic Union. He may be contacted at 3d.illustrated@gmail.com.

ACKNOWLEDGMENTS

Thanks to Elizabeth McNulty for commissioning this essay and for her enthusiastic support throughout the editorial process, to Jamie Vishwanat for her graphic design, and to Mary Reid Brunstrom, a doctoral candidate in art and architectural history at Washington University, for her research assistance. Andrew Colligan, the archivist at Missouri Botanical Garden, provided access to relevant materials at the Garden and made helpful suggestions. Dr. Peter Raven, Eugene Mackey III, Harry Richman, and Caroline Murphy De Forest all provided important historical information about the Climatron in interviews conducted in St. Louis in 2009, although any errors made here are entirely my own. An interview by Andrew Colligan with Synergetics engineer J. Forrest (Pete) Barnwell, conducted at the Missouri Botanical Garden on July 14, 2004 and archived there, was also very helpful. Mary Brunstrom also conducted interviews with Professor William Wischmeyer of Washington University and Natalie Grant. In addition to the Garden's own extensive photo archives, some additional illustrations and access to archival materials were provided by the archival staffs at the Murphy & Mackey Collection of the St. Louis Mercantile Library at the University of Missouri-St. Louis, at the James Fitzgibbon Papers at the Missouri Historical Society, St. Louis, and at the Detroit Public Library Photo Collections. Thanks to Blake Thornton of the Washington University in St. Louis Mathematics Department for his assistance on pages 84–85. Special thanks to David E. Klutho for his outstanding 3-D photography of this historic structure.

Important articles about the Climatron and related work of R. Buckminster Fuller include Robert W. Marks, *The Dymaxion World of Buckminster Fuller* (New York, 1960); "Washington University School of Architecture Geodesic Experiment, December 1954," (James W. Fitzgibbon papers, Box 15, folder 6. Missouri Historical Society Research Center Library, St. Louis); John Keasler, "Is it the model home of the future?," (*St. Louis Post-Dispatch*, Sunday, 16 January 1955); and Geoff Koch, "R. Buckminster Fuller's Legacy Here," (*St. Louis Post-Dispatch*, Sunday, January 4, 2004, B1, B5-6). The entire history of the Garden is traced in Andrew Colligan, "History of the Missouri Botanical Garden," in Elizabeth McNulty, *Missouri Botanical Garden: Green for 150 Years 1859-2009* (St. Louis, 2009), 19-65. My own *Modern Architecture in St. Louis* (St. Louis, 2004) offers an overview of the local historical and architectural context of the Climatron.

ABOVE "May festival including dances of Germanic origin," 1966.

SUSTAINABILITY

The Missouri Botanical Garden strives to make the most sustainable choices for the future of people, plants, and the planet. This book is printed on paper containing 30% post-consumer recycled content manufactured with wind power.

ENVIRONMENTAL BENEFITS STATEMENT
of using post-consumer waste fiber vs. virgin fiber

The Missouri Botanical Garden saved the following resources by printing the pages of this book on chlorine free paper made with 30% post-consumer waste.

trees	water	energy	solid waste	greenhouse gases
20 fully grown	8,767 gallons	6 million BTUs	532 pounds	1,820 pounds CO_2

Calculations based on research by Environmental Defense and the Paper Task Force.

 Mixed Sources
Product group from well-managed forests, controlled sources and recycled wood or fiber
www.fsc.org Cert no. BV-COC-080110
© 1996 Forest Stewardship Council
FSC

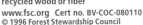

A NOTE ABOUT THE TYPE

The main body copy font is the most popular typeface in the world: **Helvetica**. Designed by Max Miedinger in 1956-58 for the German Stempel foundry, Helvetica embodies "the modern" with clean sans serif lines and international style. **Aldous vertical**, used for the headlines, was designed by Walter Huxley for American Type Founders in 1935 and became a popular commercial font in the 1950s. The body of the sidebar articles is **Sabon**, designed by Jan Tschichold in 1967, and considered a more modern form of Garamond. The pull quotes are **Market Deco**, a contemporary retro font designed by Steve Ferrera.

To discover and share knowledge about plants and their environment in order to preserve and enrich life.
—mission of the Missouri Botanical Garden.